ABC Guide
to the
Everglades

George Robinson Ph.D.

Introduction

The **Everglades** embraces a territory so expansive and varied that its character cannot be condensed into a single book. It is teeming with activity. Birds, reptiles, mammals, insects, trees and wild flowers all interact in a web of life. To protect the **Everglades**, we must all be stewards. The first step in stewardship is to be aware of what the **Everglades** has to offer. This book is an introduction for young children so that they can start to be aware of the abundance of life in this "River of Grass."

Aa is for **Alligator**

Alligators have between 74 and 80 teeth in their mouth at a time. As teeth wear down they are replaced. An alligator can go through 2,000 to 3,000 teeth in a lifetime.

Bb is for **Brown Pelican**

Pelicans do not store fish in their pouch, but simply use it to catch them and then tip it back to drain out water and swallow the fish immediately.

Cc is for **Crocodile**

American crocodiles are well-armored with tough, scaly skin. They are gray-green or olive-green with long, slender snouts, which distinguish them from their cousin, the alligator. Also unlike the alligator, the fourth tooth on the bottom jaw of the American crocodile is visible when its mouth is closed. South Florida is the only place where you can find both crocodiles and alligators.

Dd is for **Deer**

Because Key deer have lost their fear of humans, there is a serious problem with people illegally feeding them. This makes the deer more vulnerable to dog attacks or getting entangled in fences.

Ee is for **Egret**

One way to tell the difference between an egret and a heron is that egrets have black legs and herons have yellow legs. Also, egrets shake their legs while flying while herons do not shake their limbs during flight.

Ff is for **Flamingo**

The flamingo is often seen on the banks of the lake standing on one leg. The flamingo is actually sleeping when it is on one leg but the strange thing is, that only half of the flamingo is actually asleep - the half that contains the leg still standing remains active. The flamingo then swaps over so that the remaining side can get some rest and the side that was sleeping becomes active again.

Gg is for **Gallinule**

The purple gallinule, an unusual bird, is often seen walking on lily pads, supporting its weight on its very long toes, and may sometimes even be seen climbing up into low bushes in search of food.

Hh is for **Heron**

If this largest of the herons is not preening, then the great blue heron may be seen stalking as it slowly and regally hunts through the shallows.

Ii is for Ibis

The White Ibis is and always has been the most abundant wadding bird in the Everglades. It is such a signature bird that the University of Miami adopted it as its mascot.

Jj is for Scrub **Jay**

The Florida Scrub Jay lives nowhere in the world except Florida.   Acorns are its diet staple which it buries and retrieves later.

Kk is for Snail **Kite**

The snail kite is a hawk-like bird that feeds exclusively on the fresh-water apple snail. Only several hundred snail kites still live in the Everglades.

Ll is for **Lubber Grasshoppers**

Lubber grasshoppers contain toxic substances. Small mammals such as opossums have been known to vomit violently after eating a lubber, and to remain ill for several hours.

Mm is for Water **Moccasin**

The Water Moccasin or Cottonmouth eats fish, frogs, snakes, turtles, young alligators, birds (and their eggs), mice, rats, squirrels, and rabbits

Nn   is for **Night Hawk**

These birds do not make a nest. Their young are so well camouflaged that they are
seldom detected.

Oo is for **Osprey**

The osprey and owls are the only raptors whose outer toe is reversible, allowing them to grasp their prey with two toes in front and two behind.

Pp is for **Panther**

Panthers' strong hind legs allow them to leap up to 15 feet vertically and 45 feet horizontally. So few Florida panthers remain that these animals are now given special legal protection as an "endangered species."

Qq is for **Queen Butterfly**

Like those of Monarch butterflies, the larvae of Queen Butterflies feed on various species of poisonous milkweeds. The larvae accumulate the milkweed toxins, and as a result both they and the adult butterflies are quite poisonous. Birds will avoid these poisonous orange, black and white butterflies.
Photo Credit: Gene Hanson

Rr is for **Royal Palm**

The Royal Palm (Cuban Royal Palm, Florida Royal Palm) can get up to 60 – 70 feet tall and 5 -10 feet wide with a growth rate of around a foot each year.

Ss is for **Spoonbill**

The roseate spoonbill has rosy pink plumage that is accented with carmine on the wings and tail. In the United States it was almost exterminated for its fine feathers.

Tt is for **Tri-Colored Heron**

Predators like American crows, red-winged blackbirds and purple gallinules usually tend to eat and destroy the heron eggs. Turkey vultures, feral cats and raccoons also prey on the eggs and young birds.

Uu is for **United Nations**

The United Nations designated the Everglades as both a World Heritage Site and an International Biosphere Reserve.

Vv is for **Vulture**

The Turkey Vulture rides thermals in the sky and uses its keen sense of smell to find fresh carcasses. As a scavenger it cleans up the countryside one bite of its sharply hooked bill at a time, and never mussing a feather on its bald head.

Ww is for **Wood Stork**

The wood stork has earned the nickname "Preacher bird" because they insist on the practice of standing around, as if contemplating life, after eating.

A $500 reward is being offered to the first person who is able to document that South Florida rainbow snake – an animal that had been prematurely declared extinct - is still alive. The Center for Snake Conservation is offering the reward.

Yy is for **Yucca**

Dried yucca leaves and trunk fibers have a low ignition temperature, making the plant desirable for use in starting fires via friction. This parched vegetation is vulnerable to lightning strikes.

Zz   is for **Zebra Butterfly**

The zebra longwing butterfly was designated the official state butterfly of Florida in 1996. It lays its eggs on passion vine leaves. Passion vines contain toxins that are consumed by the caterpillars, which make the adult butterflies poisonous to predators.

For additional Nature Books by Dr. Robinson go to:

Naturebooksbygeorge.com

Bird Banding

ABC's of the Coral Reef